FORMS OF CONVERSION

FORMS OF CONVERSION

poems by

A L L I S O N   F U N K

Alice James Books   Cambridge, Massachusetts

Cover and book design by Sue Morrison
Typography by Arlington Graphics, Inc.

The publication of this book was made possible with
support from the National Endowment for the Arts,
Washington, D.C., and from the Massachusetts Council
on the Arts and Humanities, a state Agency whose funds
are recommended by the Governor and appropriated by
the State Legislature.

Library of Congress Catalogue Card Number 86-70728
ISBN 0-914086-64-2 (cloth)
ISBN 0-914086-65-0 (paper)

Alice James Books are published by the Alice James
Poetry Cooperative, Inc.

Alice James Books
138 Mount Auburn Street
Cambridge, Massachusetts 02138

ACKNOWLEDGMENTS

The author gratefully acknowledges the following publications in which some of the poems in this volume first appeared.

Antaeus: "New England Walls" and "The Marsh"

Columbia, A Magazine of Poetry and Prose: "The Lake"

The Georgia Review: "Trestle"

Grolier Poetry Prize 1985: "Emaki: A Scene from the Tale of Genji" and "Desire"

Pembroke Magazine: "Family Secret" (originally "Grandmother's Secret") and "At the Window"

Poetry: "The Ghost of Elinor Wylie," "Elegy" and "Forms of Conversion"

Poetry Northwest: "Georgia Power," "Twin Lakes" and "Explaining a Death to My Son"

The Seneca Review: "From the Front"

"Mirrors" originally appeared in *A Celebration for Stanley Kunitz on His Eightieth Birthday,* a book published by The Sheep Meadow Press in 1986.

I want to thank the Delaware State Arts Council for its support. I am also grateful to The MacDowell Colony and Yaddo, where many of the poems in this collection were written. Special thanks to Joel Reingold and Cleopatra Mathis for their belief in this book.

FOR MY
MOTHER AND
FATHER

CONTENTS

FORMS OF
CONVERSION

The Lake 13
Trestle 14
Georgia Power 15
Emaki: A Scene from
the Tale of Genji 16
Chrysanthemum 18
Migrations 20
At the Window 21
Explaining a Death
to My Son 22
Twin Lakes 23
Forms of Conversion 24

MIRRORS

The Stereoscope 29
Costa Rica, 1916 31
Archangel 32
From the Front 34
Family Secret 35
Blindness 36
Planting Mint 37
Mirrors 38

CROSSING

Crossing 43
Isis and Osiris 44
The House on the Cliff 46
A Bomb Explosion on a
Bus in Jerusalem 47
Elegy 48
Signs 49

MEDITATIONS
ON
A COLD ESTATE

The Marsh   53
A Distance from the Palace   54
Desire   56
The End of a Garden   57
Gulls   58
New England Walls   60
Purple Loosestrife   61
The Ghost of Elinor Wylie   63
Meditations on
    a Cold Estate   65

FORMS
OF
CONVERSION

THE LAKE

Around the lake the rhododendron bloomed.
Each bud unclenched, revealing a baby's palm.
As I awoke mornings in my cousin's room
I heard the water licking its live fur calm
Beside the creaking house. It was the summer
The hair began like webs beneath our arms
And we saw in mirrors not ourselves, but strangers
Remote and older, ones with foreign charms.
Later that year we discovered the waterfall
With its silver neck broken on the rocks. They found
My cousin down among the fish, so small,
Looking up through the lake's dark layers, drowned.
It was then the lake became as still as one
Asleep, translucent palms upturned, and stunned.

TRESTLE

You land relieved
on the next tie
as when climbing down
toward your mother's voice
you reached the safety
of another branch.
Then blossoms underfoot
fluttered off
and you felt the new leaves press
against your legs until
slipping or fearing it, you fell—
your pink arms spinning: fans.

This time it is not the grass
that reaches for you. Below,
waves open their troughs,
arrange their white sheets.
You feel the wood
beneath your feet splintering
when your mother,
with you now, says *Take my arm;*
I'm afraid.
And you hear your voice,
distant as the splash of another
falling in, say
It is not far.

GEORGIA POWER

for my brother David

You are holding it:
the jar where the dead are heaped.
Wings flattened, gray
bodies beneath the lid.
On the head and the thorax
pincer horns have let go,
just as a thumb and a forefinger
release what we've held.

At night, the leaves of rhododendron
and laurel are black.
The lakes, the mountains are buried.
But inside the power station
the lamps are all on
behind windows that stop the beetles.
They knock just once against the glass.
We find them stiff on their backs below.

Can we be of the same blood,
I, who see in the jar
every loss I have known,
and you, who with a book
bring the dead back to earth?
Beetles, *Dynastes:*
how they fight with awesome horns
to win a mate, dwell in rotting wood
and rich leaf mold, swarm to light—

it is all recorded
on the pages you've turned each year
since you stood at the foot of transformers
alive with power, telling me that no jar,
no box could keep you from hearing
the sound of wings.

15

EMAKI: A SCENE
FROM THE TALE OF GENJI

The roof has been blown away
So we see the interior of the room, a world

Of layered blues, browns and greens,
From above, as the moon would

Or the hovering dead. The steeply angled
Walls seem to converge on Genji,

Who sits, back to us, on the floor.
He might be serene, robed in pale brown,

Except for the black hat which bears him down
Like a stone. His lover, Murasaki,

Beautiful and barren, according to the story,
Is a sleeve half concealing a face, a kimono

At rest. The space between them is growing.
Outside the garden is silver and stormy,

Wind agitates the autumn grass. The tall blades
Are bending and breaking

One over the other, and finally it is
The sorrow in the grass that shows us Murasaki is dying,

For she could simply be shielding her eyes
From the evening light in order to sleep,

And Genji could be reading before turning in,
As we do without thinking.

You can tell so little of their suffering
By their faces: they could belong to anyone,

Being featureless, except for the inked brows,
The artist's last strokes over color

In a scene from a scroll
Meant to be held in your hands.

CHRYSANTHEMUM

Where birds gather in the stone bath
my friend watches the starling alone,
darkening the water.

This year April is a vessel
reflecting the coldest season,
nothing dreamed or hoped for.

Only now and then, in the early morning,
before grief claims its territory of hours—
one barren plot of land after the next—

can she believe the dogwood
a configuration of grace, her mother's wrists
and arms covered with blossoms.

But earth tilts above the green
its dark coffin, and she remembers
rabbits the dogs have dragged out of the woods,

their necks broken, sight withdrawn.
She thinks of the violence
of her mother's death, a gun.

The starling strikes the air as it flies,
then hovers in the branches, a black fruit
she eats, tasting the bitter juice

while beneath her
the earth accepts her mother
easily, fallen snow.

After a blizzard in early spring
the ground absorbs the melted snow running with salt.
It offers lilac and chrysanthemum.

MIGRATIONS

Canada geese over bone-white fields:
in autumn the constellation
moved above the house and disappeared.
I watched from the broken corn,
empty as the sky after the birds' departure.

It seemed longer than a season
that I counted the dead husks.
If you lose a child, they say,
there is no comfort
until you hear the unborn
call again for direction.

When the birds come back
it is never in clouds or arrows.
One small burden of proof,
a sparrow appears on the lawn.
Then gradually as a five-month baby
unfurls and tries the drum,
thrush, warbler, robin
and swallow congregate and sing.

Winter is still the longest season.
When the branch starts to bend
we cannot return to the warm continent
we traveled from.
But there are moments when it is enough
that my son journeyed at night and arrived.

AT THE WINDOW

In the angled light of afternoon
I watch my son
at his favorite game.
Sheer curtain before his face
he stands at the window
and looks out toward the birch,
the diamond shapes of passing cars.
Beneath each eye I see
the clear blue script of a vein.

From the beginning,
the tiny arms, peninsulas,
reached into the teeming water.
And now as I join him
to stare at the bleached walk,
silver mailbox in the road,
I am reminded
of how the sky can be a sail,
and each lean tree a mast.

EXPLAINING A DEATH
TO MY SON

Over and over you ask me for reasons.
How do the red and yellow apples
become the juice we drink?
What does bread look like in the fields?
Is the sun lost at night?
There is no end to the questioning
and my dissembling.

Your body fascinates you the most—
how your auburn hair grows
and must be harvested like the wheat.
What the branches in your wrist
signify, and when the blood will stop
when a door in your skin
opens up.

If you ask what these stones are
(under which I have so recently
buried one of our own)
I say, It is where the old people sleep.
How can I explain the separation
of birds and fruit from the trees,
my grief, to you
who believe each transformation
is a miracle?

TWIN LAKES

See yourself again
afloat in the center, demanding the grownups
look. When the oars split the lake
they brought up pads dripping lilies,
and you were certain of your power
over water. Red-spotted newts stayed
put on the bottom, and the slippery
tails of your hair dried fast in the sun.
Just as you'd learned to move your own limbs,
you mastered those wooden arms.
In their oarlocks they spoke
an octave higher than your parents
on the dock at happy hour.
That summer, rowing was all you knew,
the water showing your face.
Then you thought you could never forget
how to move forward avoiding the circles.

FORMS OF CONVERSION

Measured in miles or kilometers,
the distance we travel is the same.
A man is so many stone;
pounds do not increase him,

and the beggar who trades rubles
for dollars is still a poor soul.
Yet there are forms of conversion
we regard as miracles: coal, water and air

by some process she does not understand
become the nylons a woman removes
as carefully as a fisherman
loosens a fish from his hook.

And a man who trades one wife
for another sincerely believes
he increases his chances
for love. True—

a stereoscope can synthesize two images
of a London street, giving a viewer the illusion
of entering a foreign place. But bread
remembers its ancestors: wheat and yeast.

Copernicus did not invent our poles
of joy and grief when he found the world
was a guest in the galaxy
circulating shyly around an impressive host.

What does it take to change a person's blood
from say *A* to *O*; banish one's parents
to the last seats in a theater; separate
for all time milk from the meat?

The rabbis were rightly suspicious
when I entered the mikvah. They knew
the last breath I took before immersion
would be the air I would choke on again when I surfaced.

MIRRORS

THE STEREOSCOPE

Behind the lenses of the stereoscope I am a diver,
this antique instrument my mask,
or a pilot in goggles who, from the height
of a small plane, sees in a flash

all the members of her family
standing on the rise of a hill, or waving
from the threshold of her house.
Only their names

are above the ground now,
but I will try to bring them back with this "Perfecscope"
copyrighted eighteen ninety-three,
the year of my grandmother's birth.

Drawing from an old box a card with two views
side by side and so nearly identical
I can hardly believe the photographer moved his camera
or altered his second sight,

I wonder how she, the third daughter
of a traveling minister, came to fall in love
with the son of a mint farmer,
and, as the stereoscope calls

two images into one,
they came to live together
in my father, their son.
Here vivid in its illusion of a third dimension

is a frame of Costa Rica,
where they were married by a justice
under palms and banana trees.
But with foreground and background in focus

they are not there.
In the old black and whites
of Russia, where my grandfather waited months
barricaded in ice for a letter from his young wife,

his face is missing. They are not the couple
harvesting wheat in the turn of the century
shot of the Midwest, not quite a double
for the vested young man in Boston

approaching a woman in a stylishly feathered hat.
No trick of the lens
will bring my grandparents into relief.
I must invent them myself.

COSTA RICA, 1916

I watched the sea birds
All the way to Costa Rica —
Hands, they filled the sky waving.

Breakers against the steamer formed
The organdy ruffles of my white dress,
Wedding dress,
Packed and labeled Lafayette, Indiana.

He had written of them
And now they waded to me:
The cattle that carry
Mountains on their backs,
Gold bands strung
On their great horns.

Behind me were holidays and presents,
Indian graves where we dug up relics,
Our own cows
Still under Mother's hand.

Dusk coming on the horizon,
Cacao pods bled *sangre de toro*.
Then royal palms
Covered the faces.

On the dock the planks moving
Beneath me like the water
I had just stepped from,
Rain stoning the banana's leaves

I began to fasten the dress,
All those hooks and eyes.

ARCHANGEL

in memory of my grandfather, F.J.F.

The armistice had been declared,
but enemies wearing no uniforms
threatened the lives of our men,

so, on the last boat of the season
we slipped down the gray Thames
past Gravesend, then crept

up the east coast of England and Scotland
dodging the floating mines.
By the second of January down the black inlet

of the Kola River we piloted to Murmansk
where an ice-breaker awaited us
for the last lap of our journey.

I dreamed of the sun
as a passenger on a sled drawn by reindeer,
but nothing could move it above the horizon.

Slowly, we felt our way out of the river
and headed south into the *gorla*,
the frozen throat of the White Sea.

When we docked at Archangel
the thermometer registered thirty below
and I questioned my destiny —

how could I deliver our troops
from typhus-carrying lice, smallpox,
and other diseases more dangerous

than the Bolsheviks' artillery?
But we do not choose our orders,
and mine were as inexorable

as my memory of the bells on our *droschky*,
the two hundred miles I traveled by sled
to preach the danger of water in the coming thaw,

cholera and dysentery looming ahead of me
like a black avalanche
as inevitable as spring.

FROM THE FRONT

It will be long, my dear,
Winter —
The Arctic is ice
And you an angel
In a white field
Rising from your letters,
The linen of our bed.
It is hard to distinguish
Your face
From the clouds filming
Shapes: the torn wing
Of my tent, a gull
Buried in the flat mud,
Boots marching
In fields without men —
The crops not of my imagining
But of what accompanies survival,
As you do, making it more.

FAMILY SECRET

Alive, I could not tell you
no lullaby was sung for my first child.
In the rows of corn, down the empty halls,
I buried the truth under my tongue,
though shame is a mirror
you cannot turn from.

But now that you know
how the houses in my town closed
when I labored without a husband
to crown the waxy head,
how even her father would not look
inside the glistening cradle,

I will tell you
there was a time I thought I would not survive.
That night God brought his hand down
hard and the ax sharpened to deliver
final judgment barely missed me.

Standing at the door with floured hands,
in that terrible embarrassment of light,
I recognized the barn,
the upturned plow, how each is sentenced
to this place. My lonely child,
I have passed my fear of lightning on.

BLINDNESS

I have led him out
to the fields he has forgotten.
I have taken him out of the house
past the still of steaming mint,
beyond the barn and the garden
wild with roses. In the field
I crush mint in my hands
and smear the stain
on his eyes and mine.

Remember, I say to him,
the barn is white,
white as my neck.
A crow's wings in sodden air
are as dark as my mouth
opening on yours.
Branches of the forsythia
gilded next to the house
burn to the end
like the strands of hair
coiling to my back.

Remember, I say
with my hands on his eyes. Remember
I say to my husband who sees
only the fields
black before planting.

PLANTING MINT

note: In the past mint was planted by hand as a person was drawn by a wagon over the fields.

It isn't like the earth
as close as this.
I do not see the horse's head,
only hoofs and legs digging black.
Dirt stammers on my face.
I cannot remember the features
of those who placed me in
this hammock above the field.
Mouths open again like pocks
made by the blade
saying *plant*
and I am given the seedlings,
the wagon begins.
Face down I am dragged
inches above the loam.
My hands are closed,
won't release the mint.

I have watched others
reenter the house changed,
nails jet, hair caked.
I have dreamt of tar,
the dropped feather.
In the shadow of the wagon
there is nothing but black
swampland before and after.
Nowhere is the sky reflected,
a field of risen mint.
Open your hands cries the driver
who will not stop.

MIRRORS

The last weeks she seemed lost in a wish
to be free of us, all the blossoming
and detritus. In her darkening room
she dreamed of a place unpreyed upon,
resistant as ice is to sun in the cliffs.
But we could not accept it,
we, the family who had given her a new heart,
brilliant cloak for survival. Like the birds
we went on forever, interrupting the night
with our familiar colors and songs.
At last miniature, her thirst
unbearable, she had no voice to *remember*,
though I held my newborn for her to touch,
the closest of us to the source.

2

A life can find its way into so many
branches, into cinder, into the column
still standing. My grandmother
had a Japanese maple, its leaves
not exactly blood red. If my memory
has a color, it is the burnt purple of those leaves
as dark in April and June as in autumn.
I could say that the tree
always warned of the end, that beautiful tree
standing between the house and the road,
the house and the garden. But I resist
seeing those ragged leaves
as her hands failing, will deny
the flesh its symbol and ash.

3

The dust is everywhere,
draping the roof, resting on fences.
Covered, the bushes have nearly merged:
one full figured, the next in tow;
some with arms around one another.
I remember sleeping in her bed
under an oval frame. Inside
was a child so plump I wondered
at the weight the Madonna held.
My grandmother told me stories to sleep,
calling me daughter. If she could now
she would say the snow is a blessing
over the broken ground, so thick
are the stars not of our planting.

4

The last day I wheeled her into the sunlight,
her feet with no will of their own
brushing the lawn. She could hardly speak,
so motioned she wanted to hold my son
in the shade. Remember your cherry tree,
I said, how each season
you hung the mirrors of aluminum on its branches.
Was it their image or the sound of metal
beating metal in the wind
that frightened the birds from your fruit?
Then I could not look into her face,
seeing the cardinals, the seeds
she scattered for them,
the cherries bent around their stones.

CROSSING

CROSSING

The coastal dunes in Nuweiba moved
Beneath us: shifting sand as smooth
As wings. And inland, greater birds,
The multiple peaks of the Sinai stirred,

Awoke from ancient sleep and flew
Into the sun. Together, you
And I could cross from land to air
And on to water easily. Where

The many-fingered palm trees waved
We rented a boat with floorboards made
Of glass. And over the swirling grain
We rode to see the coral's brain

Exposed. The salted wind and our words
Steadily filled the sail. Then first
From the coral's chambers one fish darted
Straight out, newborn. And more started

Their flight for space and life, becoming
A flock — a blur of gill and wing
Enlarging until we dove and swam
Into the dark, the fathomable.

ISIS AND OSIRIS

This month I do not recognize my face
where the blue and white rivers meet.
Or my hair that grew before
dark as the cypress. Kneeling on the bank
I find a woman broken in water,
arms, hips, in fourteen pieces,
mouth full of reeds.

In the market I ask the men
if they've seen you.
They do not look up from the tables.
They do not turn from their work.
When again I ask they offer me
one word only, *widow*.

*

Yesterday I thought I saw your arms
bent among the olives. And this morning
I smelled your breath in the cumin.
Your head is a stone
in the city's wall, your muscles
the hills under flocks and vines.
In the forest I've felt
your teeth on the cones.

*

44

I summon men to my house
and when they approach
I search their hair for your curls.
I look beneath their robes. This I believe:
any man who found your chest
would exchange it for his own.
But when I see theirs
are the bodies of other men
I send them away. I will still bear you a son, Osiris.

I shall find the body your brother cut to pieces
and scattered through the kingdoms of Egypt.
I will have your heart in my basket
before the Nile rises again.

45

THE HOUSE ON THE CLIFF

after a Hittite myth

Except for the flesh, the threads were blue
to keep away evil.
And where the sky ended, saffron began:
the man's body, all perfect stitches
next to hers. In another part of the fabric,
the same, the pattern repeated and repeated.
The curtain kept out light and all its messages
so we saw only the man and woman, ourselves.

We were contented with the sewn world
and our house on the cliff,
days numerous as our bodies,
until he drew the curtain and saw
his wife and child wandering beyond the walls.
Then all the windows of the house opened at once
and I could not keep him
except by wrapping the tiny figures around his neck
until he could not see.

A BOMB EXPLOSION
ON A BUS IN JERUSALEM

The passengers might have been the white sails
so far out on a bay
they appear senseless of everything,

even the wind. Here,
where there is sand, but no water,
a wind can be so violent

it is almost evil. This blast
blew the roof off a bus
and carried metal like pages

into the air. Within, the wounded
had the look of witnesses.
They sat upright in their seats,

neither ash nor flame.
On Jerusalem's uneven hills
the twisted olive wood prefigures

mutilation. Cypresses form a treeline
of praying hands. Here
you can ride day after day

along streets like this,
past the blinding apartments,
lizards as large as a face

pinned on the stucco, four limbs splayed.
You can look and look
before you bury the view in your hands.

ELEGY

Jerusalem, 1978

To endure this place a person must hold
to dry, ungenerous soil.
With the backbone of a pine,
live with needles in her hands.

A thousand daughters and sons
and my unborn could not survive.
For nights above Jerusalem's hills
the moon diminished, erasing itself

and the face it contained.
There is a story
that birth is so easy here
a virgin conceived,

that roses take over a courtyard
naturally. But I have seen the women
out watering every evening
to bring forth only a few.

With its insistence of dust,
the desert is more honest.
And the lemon is bitter
to the seed.

SIGNS

You have no voice for grief,
only your hands
limp at your sides,
your hands closed to a fist.
It is more eloquent
than I can support
how you take your hands to the window
and slowly, very slowly,
as if at the urging of light,
open one, watching the hollow
yield to flesh.
Each finger would be a child.

A man is no different
than a woman in this:
the body changes to accommodate loss.
But let me tell you, my love,
the story of mute Zechariah,
who recovered his voice
when a son was born to him at last.

MEDITATIONS
ON
A COLD ESTATE

THE MARSH

The mist is about to give up its secret
again. Slowly, the marsh it mummified
as we slept asserts itself, cattails

and tall grass, in back of the house.
By six they have separated, body and soul.
At dawn only the geese are audible,

their foghorns sound from the half-buried pools.
Nothing will redeem their leaving,
not even the gold and cranberry

draping the stunted trees like covers
thrown over the furniture of the departed.
Our house is too close to the marsh —

in between is a splintery fence,
the bony shoulders we see over
to vapors rising each morning. Our love

may be a ghost, too.
Is there any place we have not looked
for its old body and embrace?

53

A DISTANCE
FROM THE PALACE

In Schönbrunn there is a ruin
of columns and bricks at the end of a path
that may surprise you,

having walked a distance from the great Viennese palace
with formal gardens. Broken steps,
beheaded statuary and the frieze

of astonished faces that band the walls
look vandalized. Blocks of ice
caught in the pool resemble dead fish

afloat in a stagnant pond. It is difficult
to imagine the lifted hooves of the sea
Neptune was said to rule over

and yet here he is, centered on a rise of rocks
largely obscured by moss. His naked form
is streaked and bruised in appearance,

but unbroken. A woman kneels next to him,
in her right hand what could be an oar.
Their pedestal seems a slow-moving barge.

I think she is trying to read her partner's gaze.
Every muscle in his body seems tensed
for escape, as if he is ready

to stand up and walk out
through an arch of their ruined home
toward the March trees branching like the lines

on the hand of someone you've loved.
But with one arm outstretched to her
it is just as possible he is going to speak;

he is about to explain everything.
Her breasts are as small as baby birds
tilting their beaks for food.

DESIRE

Our son spends his days
trying to name the animals.
Mornings I raise him to the window
to see the neighbor's dog;
all day he polishes the consonants
with the soft cloth of his tongue.

Every word struggled toward
means *I want.* Once named,
birds on the mobile
are touched, the wings pulled to his mouth.

You and I have almost forgotten
how our love was first spoken.
Tonight we tell each other the story
again, simply, as if we were children
and not a man and a woman who dream
of wild grass growing above the planted.

It was December in Ohio.
Your face made its own blue shadows,
it was that strong.
And mine, you said, seemed illumined
by a source far-off.

Seven years and we see ourselves
in the child alone: my eyes, your hands.
Instruct us, we ask, though we know

desire is not taught, but unlearned
as the words beginning to form
perfectly one after another
abandon the body.

THE END OF A GARDEN

for C.M.

You write that your heart has become
one of the little border stones
that marks the end of a garden.
The garden flowers, you say,
then green and fragrance fail.
December, I cut the roses to the ground
after the last bud bloomed.

Married in summer,
you filled your house with plants
and started a garden. Roses, tulips,
the sunflower ripe with seeds.
You planted vegetables:
green lace of parsley, lettuce,
and tomatoes you would can for January.
But in the early cold
you fought as the trees stiffened,
the ground began to freeze.
Happiness, like summer's claim to daylight,
ended, leaving the brick house quiet.

Where pebbles meet the disfigured plants
you stand, saying *This is how far the garden grew,*
no farther, no longer.
As clouds condense and fall,
so surely erasing the leaves, your own cold hands,
it seems you will spend your life
recording the weather: summer, then snow.
How a tree in the yard
is gold for only a day.
Someone opens a locket,
showing for a moment the woman and man,
then closes it, tightening the latch.

GULLS

During these weeks of unyielding rain
when good weather should have arrived
but hasn't, I listen to the gulls
that have strayed miles from the sea.
Theirs is the octave of an unoiled door
opening and closing until I feel

I could be in another place,
a corner poorly lit,
where men muscle fish
and ice into crates before dawn.
One summer you chose this backbreaking work,
then gave it up, fearing you would acquire
the blank eye of the haddock and cod
piled one on top of the other.

Barely twenty and tourists,
how were we to understand this town of rock
set against storms that rob the nets,
sea smoke which makes a mist
out of men over water?

Now work is the only thing fixed in our lives,
predictable as the men in Gloucester
leaving their homes for those fishhouses.
At night I hear you panting
in your sleep, still working.
Does anything come to rest,

the gulls circling above the flooded ground?
I would like to trust that one story
can be exchanged for another
and another, that inspiration
may still be possible.

NEW ENGLAND WALLS

They announce where one man's property begins
and ends. In New England you find them everywhere,
you said, ringing the acres of devil's paintbrush

and Queen Anne's lace, flush with the birches.
I told you it puzzled me that these walls did not budge,
flat rocks and triangles over round stones

that should have relented
during the hard winters here, the spaces
between them unsealed. We talked about our marriages,

which had hardened into mystifying shapes.
All boundaries are arguments
against passion, but one night

before taking the paths to our separate rooms
we stood amazed before a field
so flooded with moonlight it shone,

as if covered with snow. It was June,
the air was close, and I was drowsy,
but the confusion of seasons unearthed a tenderness.

Couldn't we have called it accidental
if we had dissolved among the little animals
and the grass? Why, in your black clothes,

did you come steadily back into focus,
a tree that would not blossom
even briefly?

PURPLE LOOSESTRIFE

*"There was one shrub in particu-
lar...that bore a profusion of purple
blossoms, each of which had the
lustre and richness of a gem..."*
*(from "Rappaccini's Daughter"
by Nathaniel Hawthorne)*

The name must be the invention of a half-mad botanist
more in love with words

than the nature of corollas and stamens.
In my book of wild flowers I search

for a term that will allow me to understand
the stalk as tall as a woman

with heart-shaped leaves and reddish-
purple blossoms for what it is

to the eye alone. But found, *Lythrum
salicaria* still blurs against my will

in this flooded zone, neither sea
nor its consolation of solid ground

until the purple glow spreads
as far as the horizon.

Hawthorne, in neighboring Salem,
called his terrible flower only "some strange peril,"

yet it rooted in its victim:
a woman whose desire was poison.

I have read more than one warning
of this plant which broken by wind or water

still spends its hundred thousand seeds,
will root, thrive and overtake the cattails

populations of birds
and small animals consume to survive.

But believing in another version
which invests *Loosestrife* with the power

to stop bleeding, I approach the beauty,
caring not what I must sacrifice to acquire it —

how I must leave my house
to enter the moist and garish world

of the swamp where snakes circle underfoot
and there's no seeing before or behind,

where the pools mirror the wild
and driven faces of the weed

which leans over me, insists upon its name
and adds, *whore.*

THE GHOST OF ELINOR WYLIE

There is a legend Elinor Wylie was so jealous
of Edna St. Vincent Millay she haunts writers at night,
inquiring "Am I beautiful?" of women
and sleeping men. This evening her ghost
is a net over my face, demanding my breath and answer,
the confirmation of beauty

I am always ready to grant to other women;
to the birch trees illuminating at night
the whole wooded road, ghostly
and devious as swans; to the ferns whose leaflets answer
each other from opposite sides of a stem, jealous
exquisite twins. Beauty

and its failure surround me. Unbeautiful
now, my mirror overflows with the ghosts
of Edna and Elinor, a host of young women
who used to charm. And because no dream can answer
this doubt, I implore the whirlpool of a man at night
to erase the sad boundaries of the self. How jealous

the moon is of the sun all those nights
her face is changing to a woman's
in her middle years, diminishing until her beauty
is wasted and she is a single ray, less than a ghost,
a spine cursed by her answer:
the new moon will be her daughter. What jealous

shades must I turn to, the beautiful
ferns, as delicate as underclothing, the ghostly
mist which obscures the fields at night,
the fireflies that are women,
too, burning the candles of their sex, as jealous
as all the unloved. Who will answer me?

MEDITATIONS ON A
COLD ESTATE

1

This snow reminds me of the letter
I have not written you.
Mid morning, sun parts the shaggy pines,
illuminating the tracks of birds,
faint, watermarks,
so unlike the strident prints
my boots have left behind.
The words *I hate you,* said a novelist,
can ruin the surface
affection may have polished smooth,
but sometimes I can find no others
to explain the distance I have put between us:
my hoop of flames.

2

I understand why snow is said to "blanket,"
for it invites our dreams and separate sleep.
Since I've been away, the hours
have been my allies and my own inventions —
but was it you who hung
the painting in my single room?
I admire the sky that is the dark blue
tip of a matchstick. And in the paler water,
the weightless rowboats. My favorite is the one
the artist singled out, giving its hollow
the brilliance of a dome.
But it is not art where the water ends
and the three figures on the dock
with their backs to me are walking:
the brittle green mother
with red and blue children.

3

Go away, I said, invoking the charity of sleep.
But I heard the sound again
in a house empty of other sleepers.
I struggled to give the voice
a passive shape, any one — vase or lamp —
before, finally, I recognized the syllables
of the Great Horned Owl that inhabits these woods.
Even then, the spirit would not stay on its branch;
it insisted on coming in.
Or was it I who opened the window
in the coldest month of the year
to join the bird
in her passionless call for her mate?

4

At the entrance to these woods is a brooding mansion
with a stained glass pane. I stand there
remembering sex and the saints in the walls
of a great cathedral consenting,
the rose which was a window and my own flower
shimmering. They are forever mingled,
awe and the recollection of my virginity
lost in a foreign city

as now, before me, cut glass is joined color to color.

Clearing a web of snow from my face
I look at the actual man and woman in the window.
He has the chivalrous posture of a hero
holding a lover in his arms.
The woman's head is thrown back in a swoon,
I think, but she becomes so quiet
I worry her pulse into a broken timepiece.
Then it is clear what is wrong:
where the lovers should have eyes
and mouths for one another
they are snow.

5

A formal garden is more formal in winter;
even the grass is converted to marble.
Think of the estate in summer:
the fountain restored to full height,
the blue iris out of its closet,
grapes on the vines.
I have asked you for impossible gifts,
wanting to be the idolized wife
whose name is chiseled
near the iron door that swings in the wind.

6

I walked a long time with no sense of direction
down a road shadowed by pines,
looking for a lake as invisible
as what a woman carries within her
nine months but cannot see.
I walked so long I began to doubt its existence,
as the woman, a little older
and married to one man ten years,
questions what she thought once
was permanently housed in her heart.

I want to send you a letter now,
though I still hardly know what to write.
Only this: what I had searched for
was something so deep no one
could swim to the end of it.
When finally I found the lake
it was simply the absence of trees
and another acre of snow.
I might have easily passed it
if not for a muffled clue:
a stream of water had escaped
from under the covered ice,
and flowing downhill, it sounded like rain.

POETRY FROM ALICE JAMES BOOKS

Thirsty Day   Kathleen Aguero
In the Mother Tongue   Catherine Anderson
Personal Effects   Becker, Minton, Zuckerman
Backtalk   Robin Becker
Legacies   Suzanne E. Berger
Afterwards   Patricia Cumming
Letter from an Outlying Province   Patricia Cumming
Riding with the Fireworks   Ann Darr
ThreeSome Poems   Dobbs, Gensler, Knies
33   Marjorie Fletcher
US: Women   Marjorie Fletcher
No One Took a Country from Me   Jacqueline Frank
Forms of Conversion   Allison Funk
Natural Affinities   Erica Funkhouser
Without Roof   Kinereth Gensler
Bonfire   Celia Gilbert
Permanent Wave   Miriam Goodman
Signal::Noise   Miriam Goodman
Romance and Capitalism at the Movies   Joan Joffe Hall
Raw Honey   Marie Harris
Making the House Fall Down   Beatrice Hawley
The Old Chore   John Hildebidle
Impossible Dreams   Pati Hill
Robeson Street   Fanny Howe
The Chicago Home   Linnea Johnson
From Room to Room   Jane Kenyon
Streets after Rain   Elizabeth Knies
Dreaming in Color   Ruth Lepson
Falling Off the Roof   Karen Lindsay
Temper   Margo Lockwood
Black Dog   Margo Lockwood
Shrunken Planets   Robert Louthan
Animals   Alice Mattison
The Common Life   David McKain
The Canal Bed   Helena Minton
Openers   Nina Nyhart
Night Watches: Inventions on the Life of Maria Mitchell   Carole Oles
Wolf Moon   Jean Pedrick
Pride & Splendor   Jean Pedrick
The Hardness Scale   Joyce Peseroff
Curses   Lee Rudolph
The Country Changes   Lee Rudolph
Box Poems   Willa Schneberg
Against That Time   Ron Schreiber
Moving to a New Place   Ron Schreiber
Contending with the Dark   Jeffrey Schwartz
Changing Faces   Betsy Sholl
Appalachian Winter   Betsy Sholl
Rooms Overhead   Betsy Sholl
From This Distance   Susan Snively
Deception Pass   Sue Standing
The Trans-Siberian Railway   Cornelia Veenendaal
Green Shaded Lamps   Cornelia Veenendaal
Old Sheets   Larkin Warren
Tamsen Donner: a woman's journey   Ruth Whitman
Permanent Address   Ruth Whitman